LIVING
beyond the
TREMORS
~
MY JOURNEY WITH PARKINSON'S

CAROLINE GILBERT

Living Beyond The Tremors
Caroline Gilbert

All rights reserved
First Edition, 2024
© Caroline Gilbert

No part of this publication may be reproduced, or stored in a retrieval system, or transmitted in any form by means of electronic, mechanical, photocopying or otherwise, without prior written permission from the author.

ISBN: 978-1-3999-9641-9

Dedication

To Bill, my friend and steadfast companion through the challenges of Parkinson's. Your strength and encouragement were invaluable and your memory remains a source of inspiration.

Contents

Introduction 1
Begins the journey with Parkinson's, reflecting on early symptoms and diagnosis.

Essence of Parkinson's 3
Captures the impact of symptoms and the daily battles with resilience.

In The Beginning 5
A look back at early signs of Parkinson's and the path ahead.

Reflection 1 7
A reflection on adapting routines and finding solace in brief moments of normalcy.

Living with Parkinson's 9
Questions and frustrations about living with the disease's complexities.

Me and Parki 11
Personifies Parkinson's, blending humour with the stark reality of symptoms.

Me and Parki Through the Years 16
A journey through stages of Parkinson's, emphasizing resilience.

A New Normal 18
Accepting Parkinson's as a life partner, finding humour along the way.

A Simple Shower or Not 20
The unexpected struggles of daily tasks, with humour and frustration.

Reflection 2 24
A day's cycle of medications, pain, and exhaustion.

A Parkinson's prayer 26
A prayer for peace and resilience.

Growing Weaker 27
Facing physical decline with determination.

I Fell Today… 30
Recounting a fall and finding strength despite vulnerability.

Constipation…on the Move or Not 32
A humorous look at the frustrating reality of managing constipation with Parkinson's.

Yellow Seats Amidst Covid Shortages 33
A light-hearted look at a unique side effect of Parkinson's medication.

Reflection 3 34
An introspective piece on the mental and emotional toll of Parkinson's.

Don't ask me to punctuate 36
A whimsical exploration of the difficulties of typing and writing due to Parkinson's

The Victims of PD … 37
A powerful dedication to those who live with Parkinson's, capturing the hidden struggles.

Reflection 4 43
An introspective piece on the mental and emotional toll of Parkinson's.

A Poem While You Wait at The Airport 45
A plea for understanding in public spaces.

Waiting in the Supermarket Queue 47
Struggles for independence in simple tasks.

A Visit to The Doc 50
Challenges in communicating the complexities of Parkinson's to healthcare providers.

Reflection 5 53
Reflecting on years with Parkinson's and the journey's complexity.

Another Year Over 55
Marking the passage of time, holding hope for a cure.

The Parkinson's Shuffle 57
A humorous "dance" with Parkinson's, celebrating resilience.

A Currant Bun… 59
Wishing Parkinson's could be given up as easily as a treat.

Caroline Gilbert diagnosed with Parkinson's Disease October 2005 aged 47. Author Photograph by Melody Grisaffi, in Brittany, France.

Introduction

It was October 2005 when I first entered the Department of Neurology at St. Michael's Hospital, Dun Laoghaire. My intention, to seek an explanation for the diminishing ability to write, even my own name. A fundamental part of everyday life that seemed to be slipping away. The only other observation came from my family who were concerned that my writing had become smaller and increasingly difficult to read. "Is your husband with you?" the Professor asked, in a tone that signalled something was about to be revealed. Always preferring to handle my own health matters independently I calmly replied, "No". What followed was a ten-minute examination, a diagnosis of Parkinson's disease, advice on where to gather more information and a prescription which I admit to not taking until a month later, afraid that it might somehow damage my brain. Realistically though, I was later informed that the Dopamine levels in the brain will have reduced by eighty percent prior to the first symptom appearing. So, nineteen years later, and I have battled my way through an ever-changing kaleidoscope of unbelievable symptoms and side effects, which I have tried to document for my family. However, with an estimated ten million people worldwide currently suffering from Parkinson's, five percent of which like myself, are diagnosed under the age of fifty, along with the alarming statistic of this illness doubling over the next twenty years, sharing my story seems more important. Parkinson's remains the second leading neurodegenerative disease after Alzheimer's. Even though any two people's symptoms may never be the same, they may be similar, so for those who are carrying this illness and would just like to compare notes, those who just wish to learn more, or for no other reason than something to read, the following are some of my personal experiences living with PD.

Note from the Author

Punctuation is a luxury I cannot afford. Life with Parkinson's has taught me that each word I manage to write is a victory. There is beauty in the struggle, in capturing the truth without worrying over perfection. These words may be unpolished, but they are raw and real, written in moments when I am lucky enough to find the strength. If my punctuation falters, understand it is because I am focused on something bigger, sharing my journey with you.

Essence of Parkinson's

I started to talk and stopped midstream
What was I saying? What did I mean?
What was the topic? What was the suggestion?
Can you remind me what was the question?
PD has hit me slowly, surely, seeping,
My life source depleting,
Making me shuffle, making me shake,
Making me sleep, keeping me awake,
Making me tired, making me weak,
Making me misunderstood when I speak

Swaying this way, swaying that,
Tripping up, falling flat,
Making me fidgety, making me slow,
Making me freeze, stopping the flow,
Toes curling, limbs stiffening,
Legs twisting, hands fisting,
Body pain, weight gain,
Eyesight failing, hallucinating,
Back crumbly, voice mumbly,
Sleep deprivation, hesitation, constipation, agitation,
Anxiety, sadness, BLOODY GOING MADNESS

Not hearing what I've said, urgency in bed,
Finishing, falling, failing, freezing,
Mayhem, clutter, confusion for no reason,
Nodding off, shouting out,
Coming round…what's that about?
People staring, anger flaring,

They not knowing, not caring
Will I scream? Will I shout?
Will I let these frustrations out?
If I told them what PD's about,
Will it make a difference? I doubt

Try, inform, unite, fight,
Pin this cure down, kick it out of sight,
For it knows no boundaries, holds no shame,
Continuing to strike again and again
Will you be next? Yes, you well may,
So please stand together on World Parkinson's Day….

In The Beginning

It's been sixteen years
Since I started living with PD
As I look back, I am reminded of how it affected me
Just now and then, a twitch in my thumb
Occasionally going a little bit numb
But not for long and I thought, "No harm"
But slowly it progressed down my arm
It felt heavy and weak and hard to twist
And my hand would go into a tight fist

Then someone said, "Why look so sad"
I thought I was fine was I going mad
Then sleepless nights became my norm
Just the start of a pending storm
With fidgety legs I could neither sit nor stand
My right arm ceased to move with my hand
There were times when I would fall asleep
While sitting chatting to friends
Only to wake and say something completely out of zen

Anxiety took hold and my fear was high
I gave up driving with little reason why
I couldn't do one thing without moving to another
Leaving a trail of undone clutter
I never seemed to finish things
Only reach halfway
Before moving on to something else
That's a symptom they say

But my leg is in constant twisting
My toes curling inward my hands fisting

I get confused when there's too much talk
And without medication I cannot walk
Then I need help to move and put me into bed
Again in the morning to help me rise instead
I take life one day at a time
Some days are bad some days are fine
It's all in the timing of the pills
Whether you move or stay still
Yet we have to keep going we cannot give in
It's a struggle to keep up but we can't let him win
So as much as it hurt's we have to stay strong
We live off our memories before things went wrong

Life has been reduced to one of medication
Mixed in with some time and dedication
But to those people whose lives have been changed
Whose paths have been altered
From what was originally arranged

Stay strong have faith get through each day
And let laughter help cut those struggles away
If not you will be consumed with darkness and fear
Depression and sadness will be ever near
Rather hold your head high with a smile on your face
And carry this illness with dignity and grace
Be remembered by your loved ones
For the person they've known
Before PD came uninvited and made you, his home…

Reflection 1

I sit here amongst an amalgamation of various papers, scribbles, notes barely readable all that's left of my years of methodical book-keeping, my well-kept records of a forgotten era. I cannot seem to function in that mind-set any longer, instead days start as they end... little bundles of my endeavours everywhere, unaccomplished and incomplete.

My right hand is locked into its own agenda, and my left leg continues to go around and around simultaneously, the inner muscles twisting and turning until I feel as if they will soon snap. My medication, that awful time-consuming affliction is due and my body cringes at the thought of having once again to release those multi-coloured tablets from their sealed confines not one...two... three... but four, each doing what I don't know but yet I swallow them. I feel no immediate difference but after a while the twisting stops, my hand unlocks and stiffly stretches and I'm able to walk without dragging my legs.

I can enjoy momentarily working in the garden, the sun on my face, the peace and tranquillity of being on my own. I am myself again if only for a short while. I am tired now. I sit and sleep takes me unexpectedly. Awakening then in the same position, I stand up slowly, gently loosening the rest of my joints as I rise. I can do no more today, yet I found great contentment in those special moments at one with myself and nature. I drag my feet indoors, my left ankle turns outward and pains me as if it were twisted. What message is my brain relaying to my unsuspecting body and where next will be its victim?

The day moves on and the night draws in but no sleep passes my way. Instead, my misinformed body is convinced its daytime and I stay up through the night moving from one task to another. My only consolation from past experience is that I will sleep the following evening. And then, in the morning when I awake, stiffly rising from the bed, slowly dragging myself to meet the needs of the day I will begin to strip those multi-coloured tablets from their confines and wait and wait… until they give the green light to go and I move forward…

Living with Parkinson's

Why do I wake up exhausted
Why can't I jump out of bed
Why does it take hours
For me to do normal things instead
Why are my fingers so stiff
Why are my legs so weak
Why do I lose conversation
Leaving people at a loss when I speak
Why can't I sort stuff anymore
Why do I just shuffle things around
Why do I feel so uncomfortable
Why do my feet hug the ground
Why does my back ache when I stand too long
Why can't I rise without swaying
Why can't I write my own name at times
What is my body saying
Did I do something wrong in the past
Did I bump my head, or what
Did I eat something that was sprayed
Or was it the genes I got
Should I not have had fillings in my teeth
Should I not have drunk water from a well
Did I have too much trauma in my life
Pray, how does one tell
Research keeps listing these causes
But a cure is what we're about
They say there's one just around the corner
Then leave us all in doubt
How is it they can travel to space
Yet can't fix a brain
Is there some underlying loyalty

To the pharmaceutical chain
Time is passing so quickly
Yet my movements are ever slowing
I look around me in the waiting room
And see where my destiny is going
The tablets won't work forever
And my smile will soon be lost in a frown
My voice will not be understood anymore
And my words too difficult to write down
So, on this special PD day
To all who have a choice
Be mindful of its existence
And give this illness a voice
Stay informed and demand a cure
Give it all you can give
Take heed while you're able
And be prepared to really live
For I don't suppose I'm at my end
But I'm finding it hard to cope
My numerous afflictions ever increasing
Is there really any hope
Yet this is how he wears you down
Until you can't take much more
Hoping you'll give up the fight
Too exhausted to keep the score
But at certain given moments
When the sun shines on your face
Or someone makes you laugh
And you're in a happy place
These are the times that strengthen your mind
Gives you hope and energy within
Enough to say, "God damn it
I'm going to hang on and kick this thing".

Me and Parki

There is a disease they call Parkinson
Its symptoms are very clever
They appear slowly and silently
But grow and stay forever
It's been with me now nine years
Add two years more fermenting
The honeymoon's drawing near an end
And I fear there is no relenting
We've been asked to mark Parkinson's disease
In whichever way we're able
So, I'm giving my two pennies' worth
And putting it out there on the table

One day as I was pouring tea
A rattle of the cup alerted me
To what I thought was a nerve gone queer
Never thought there was anything to fear
And whatever way I held a plate
That little shake my hand would make
The same as when holding a pen
Just my right one now and then
But slowly my writing seemed to go
From fast and big to small and slow
What started off so tidy and neat
Became a scrawl at the end of the sheet

It never bothered me too much at the time
Still thought all was fine
Until I started a college degree

Living Beyond The Tremors

Then problems really hit me
I began to write the lectures down
But my arm and hand would not go round
As others sped across the page
I couldn't get past the title stage
So, on to the computer I did try
But my finger couldn't right-click
And I didn't know why

Such everyday actions, like ABC
Were ceasing to work and crippling me
Anxiety came next and said hello to me
And made himself at home on my knee
Little did I know he had been biding his time
Just the next symptom along the line
Yes, each one brought another
They came plenty and quick
But the strong lingering smells
Were the hardest to stick
For whenever a strong smell
Floated through the air
For days in my nose
That strong smell would repose

To come back another day
As strong as ever
Oh! that Parkinson was clever
Forever in your airways
Forever in your mouth,
Afraid to speak in case those
damn smells would just pop out.
Or if you started to do a task
The concentration would go so fast

So onto another one you would flow
Until a dozen tasks were on the go
Do you finish them
No, not ever
You just put into bags
Visiting them whenever

And when all are in bed
You're up full of beans
Night is day
To your brain it seems
But wait there's more
Your fingers keep locking
One leg is going round and round
Something shocking
You're walking with your knees bent
Your ankle thinks it's twisted
Your knuckles are swollen and lumpy
Your hands are stiff and fisted
Your neck and spine get weak
You try to move your feet
They talk about the cog-wheel reaction
It feels more like you're in traction

But that auld Parki he's so clever
He changes symptoms like the weather
So an ongoing mixture of this and that
Can keep you up or knock you flat
Then just as you thought
Things couldn't get madder
You're in the supermarket
And you just can't gather
What were you there for

What will you get, hours later
And you're not finished yet

Then fumbling at the checkouts
You're trying to pack
But it's all made worse
By the queues at your back
Feeling so awkward
And very, very slow
You'd love to shout out
And let everyone know
"I've Parkinson, I can't help it
I'm not what you see
I'm really quite clever
This is not the real me"

And just because you don't see
Me shake or sway
It's because the meds are
Keeping those symptoms at bay
But it's the ones inside
That no one can see
That are slowly stopping me
From being me
So if I look around
With a silent plea
Please sense my need
And help me
For that Parki pack
Weighs heavy on my back
And like a clinging vine
It will grow in time

But keep looking for me
Beneath that weight and clutter
I'll be there amidst the
Shakes, the swaying, and the stutters
The indecisiveness, anxieties
The trails of unfinished tasks
The endless sleepless nights
And that miserable Parki mask
And I'll be laughing like I used to
And carrying the same dreams
I will still be that same person
I will not be what I seem…

Me and Parki Through the Years

Well if you're wondering how we're doing Parki and me
I'd say we have definitely reached stage three
There's five in all or so they say
After that who knows which way
My left leg continues to cramp throughout the day
Tightening the muscles like a snake around its prey
Toes curling inwardly set the nerves alight
And stiff hands lock around fingers that are out of sight
I sleep wherever I lay my head
And unlike others it constitutes my bed
Oh, how I reminisce the sanctity of night
And the eight hours of oblivion tucked up tight

The bags are still full and all about
The contents of which without a doubt
Have been forgotten but what can I do
When my brain wanders on to something new
But still the shaking has not appeared
I've been thus saved from that which we fear
Except when standing in a shower or bath
Then my legs and back take on a trembling wrath
It's hard to find the hours in one full day
To do all I want in my own old way
I've had to accept a new way of coping
In order to fight against the stillness of moping

Yes, even when my legs feel they have weights
And my eyes close and my body aches
I have moments of joy like the sun on my skin

Or a soft breeze blowing, warm and thin
The changing seasons intertwined
All bring focus to my mind
So I'll continue to refuel my brain
With that Pinky-Brown tablet that keeps me sane
Until such time as it works no more
Then I'll pray that there's a backup somewhere in store
To prevent this imprisonment of my limbs
And the indescribable feeling it brings

This is my journey walk with me if you will
Bear witness to my decline until I am still
Laugh with me through each stage it brings
Keep me sane, be my wings
For this is life and how else can we measure
The size of that contentment or laughter we so treasure
Unless we have a baseline to compare its weight
A burden to carry… an alternative fate

So, lift up proud and strong
Kick this leech where it belongs
Laugh until your sides grow sore
Explode those toxins 'till they damage no more
For if one morning I were to wake
And joyous laughter we did forsake
Then I would surely drown in sorrow
For what would be left for tomorrow
Then journey with me on this road
As I battle whatever this illness unfolds
Become an advocate, be a voice
Parkinson doesn't give you a choice
He's lurking around looking for prey
Let's hope it's not you today….

A New Normal

It's been 10 years now since I got the news
That day I recall too well
Just a few steps up and down the room
And a twist of my arm, he could tell
"You have Parkinson's my dear" he stated
So clear, forthright and straight
No pussyfooting, edging, or easiness
yet what was the reason to wait
"It's a neurological movement disease
It's something that won't go away
We can give you medication
As it progresses from day to day"
I never blinked an eyelid
No words came from my mouth
Just a thank you for his time
And a reason for my strife

Though the oddest thing I never shook
nor did fear come to my mind
Just acceptance of a name recalled
From way back in time
Yes, I remember that customer clearly
It was difficult for him to walk
I supported him with cushions
Listening as he tried to talk
I poured his tea, I stirred his cup
I turned the handle, making it easier to pick up
I sensed his discomfort which I tried to ignore
Acknowledging the man he was before
I sympathized with his wife

I expressed my concern
I held her hand and listened
As she looked so tired and worn

Now I have that same disease
As I walk back to the train with silent ease
My only thoughts for my husband I send
Whose caring now will know no end
On my journey home I make that call
I laugh as I tell him my newest downfall
So he laughs too as he knows I'm okay
And the laughter continues every day
For laughter is that common bond
A leveler in life's frustrating pond
A natural catharsis that dilutes our fears
A channel to journey the prevailing years

So, laugh all you can my fellow friends
And let its peaceful calm your anxieties mend
Let your eyes shine and lift your pain
Reflect in them your true self again
They'll hear your laugh along with mine
The common denominator for all time
A smooth path to consume our woes
An internal lullaby on this journey we go
So, laugh all you can and laugh some more
It's the greatest gift we have in store
It will lighten your life and treat you well
It will spread and multiply wherever you dwell
Forget what life brings don't live in the past
Lift up that burden and move forward fast
Life is for living so seize every day
Continue to live and just laugh all the way….

Living Beyond The Tremors

A Simple Shower or Not

I tried to have a shower today
I thought I would be okay
But it took so long to gather bits
Nothing was going my way
Of course, when the toilet came into view
I simply had to go
Which took a good while before success
These things I'm sure you know
But what do you do when the toilet roll falls
And unravels on its journey to be free
Okay for some folks to grab it quick
Not happening to those with PD

I was delayed once more by my PJ's
Refusing to drop to the ground
My feet pushing the legs down
Like a marching band without sound
At last I was ready to go
So gingerly in I stepped
I tried to pull closed the quadrant door
And I could have nearly wept
For no matter how hard I tried
That door refused to budge
That is until I gave it
A rather heavy-handed nudge

To my alarm it fell away
And landed 'tween knee and shoulder
As I tried to rescue the situation

I was quickly growing colder
How do I grab onto the bars
When a door is laying on my side
While reaching for the shower gel
Which somehow onto the floor did glide
And where had the towel gone amongst all this muddle
Well it had fallen from the remaining door
And landed in a big puddle

So there I be between land and sea
One side of a quadrant door laying on my knee
A wet towel my only protection
The shower door missing one section
At this stage I'm shivering
My lips are quivering
No one hears me shout
The towel had gone AWOL
The panel on freefall
I just wanted to get out
My PD was starting to overload
And freeze zone was entering the equation
My brain was disconnecting from my body
Not allowing me to move despite persuasion
A simple shower that's all I asked
Why is it such a big task
It's that blasted PD he's still haunting me
Driving me crazy each day
Adding hurdles I can hardly cope with
Yet I can't run away

Everything is becoming complicated
Major issues are beginning to show
I'm starting to be less independent

How much further will I be let go
Yet I have to accept my fate
Like those who have gone before
I know I'm into my eighteenth year
But I'd like another eighteen more
So I shoved that panel door into space
And stood there in all my glory
After shouting for help
A towel eventually squeezed through the doorway

A lovely hand towel, nothing more
At least it had pretty flowers
How long it would take to dry myself
You could be talking hours
In the meantime I was frozen and numb
And knew I had to act
The shaking was increasing
But would my dignity remain intact
I wrapped the wet towel around my waist
And must have looked a sight
With what looked like a flowery teacloth
held against me tight

I opened the door and shuffled across
To the bedroom as fast as I could go
As PD only knows quick, freeze or slow
And in between he hinders you
By making things go wrong
It makes him happy to think
He's so powerful and strong

So, if there's a lesson in this story
Be prepared to catch him out
A simple thing like a shower
He really can mess about
But I'll get my revenge when
My bathroom is rearranged
No shower door just a nonslip floor
Toilet rolls that can't escape
Towels all stacked up ready to take
A seat should I get weak and no soap
Or wet towels under my feet

Oh yes, I'll have the last laugh
He won't win next time around
I'll be prepared in every way
And stand my solid ground
He thinks he knows me well by now
But I think I know him more
And I won't let that happen again
I'll be keeping score
I'll not move until my medication says
Ready, steady, now go,
And hopefully, Mr. Parky, will go down
With the overflow....

Reflection 2

I get up from my bed and face the day. I take some breakfast and dress. By this time, I start to feel the familiar return of that inner ache across my lower back like a wave stretching further and further over the sand. It fills each crevice of my spine and draws all my strength back with its tide. I start to shuffle, barely able to lift my legs, like someone has brushed the soles of my feet with a sticky, tar-like substance making each step laboured. Pulling my feet upwards, I try to break free but to no avail the tar remains, and I feel myself stagger.

So at 10 am I reach once again for more dopamine just one tablet this time, but enough to melt that sticky mass and free my limbs for a few more precious hours whereby I can continue with everyday tasks. Will this be a good day? What will I achieve? Should I rest for an hour until my limbs are truly free, or shall I try to shuffle my way through whatever I can? Not wanting to waste time, I attempt to start something, but exhausted, my body soon screams, "Wait".

It's 2 pm, and already my back and legs are starting to inwardly shake. Once again a dull pain spreads up through my spine and grabs at my shoulders, making it impossible to stand even for a moment. That tide is slowly creeping in again and so I take more dopamine, hoping to reduce its power and stop it in its stride.

Again, I am allowed a window of freedom, but the day is long and by 6 pm, I start to waiver and ultimately refuel, weary of Parki's constant onslaught. The invisible symptoms of exhaustion, twisting, anxiety, pain and what remains of my executive function at odds with the visible ones of stiffness and shuffling and I long to take to my bed. But I hesitate knowing that my leg will twist and turn and for relief, I will have to hold both foot and leg in a continuous position of flexion, the calf and hip muscles held taut until they ache. The alternative is to place my leg under a heavy weight but even then, I am conscious of its inner writhing.

My 10 pm top-up is due, that final medication which ensures movement to the rest of my body through the night. And even though my leg is on system overload it is a small price to pay for the feeling of normality before I close my eyes. For I have witnessed sleepless nights hovering around each room, those crawling restless legs eventually taking me to the roads until dawn. I have glimpsed momentarily the frightening destruction of my body without the medication and have cried when my feet would not follow my brain's instruction.

Yet I must remain upbeat rather than let Parki take me down as he thrives on negativity. And to all who suffer his wrath, it is a lonely illness born inwardly as not to bother, laughed outwardly as not to worry, and faced bravely with uncertainty. For what use is a tap without water, a car without fuel, a brain without dopamine? One dependent on the other and without which, one will surely cease.

A Parkinson's prayer

Was it you who sat with me through the night
When all were asleep and out of sight
Was it you who walked with me through each room
When the crawling irritation in my legs did spoon

Was it you who watched over me while I slept
Exhausted from walking when my legs would not rest
Was it you who then gently opened my eyes
To wake me from my makeshift paradise

Was it you who waited so patiently
While the medication released me free
Was it you who then guided me through the day
Walking behind me all of the way

Was it you who opened my mind
To speak of my illness through poetic lines
Was it you who gifted my every word
In order for my voice to be heard

Was it you who promised to leave me never
When my purpose in life ceased forever
Was it you that laid my mind to rest
And told me I had done my best

Then it was you who gently took my hand
Walked me to that promised land
It was you who said to me my endeavours had ceased
And blessed me with an everlasting peace…

Growing Weaker

I'm growing weaker I have to say
Losing a part of myself each day
Every piece of me feels disconnected
PD once again has me affected
I was one step in front of him but
Now he's wormed his way ahead
If only I could suck him out
And stamp on him till dead
But no, that little blighter refuses to move
As if some higher status he's trying to prove
I'm not sure what more he wants from me
He's destroyed everything I had
But the grip on my body he still holds firm
And he won't let go… how sad
Now he's made me have a fall
Which could have killed me dead
I can hear him laughing at me
Because that's how he is fed

My jeans I was trying to put on
From an upright position
But a second later I found myself
In a downward transition
I grabbed one side of the bedtable
To save me from going south
But forgot there were painted floorboards
And the wheels just slid on out
The other end of that table took a westward route
And slammed into my neck in quick pursuit

As my body travelled into space
I felt fluid dripping down my face
Immediately I thought I'd severed a vein
And my life I wasn't going to regain again
So I placed a hand gingerly on my face
Cold tea replaced the blood I traced
Then Jim came running and helped me up
Inciting there could have been hot tea in that cup
One look in the mirror revealed a neck of red
Replaced the next day by black and blue instead
If that was a human he'd be arrested and jailed
Yet as much as he's blamed he can never be nailed

Now I've recovered I'm awaiting more of the same
To that PD alien, it's only a game
He can take over your body and control it from within
Making you trip and fall at whim
But I have his back covered
And he's in for a shock
For one of these days they'll find a lock
Big enough to hold a door
Where we can incarcerate him forevermore
And with it he can take his tremors and shakes
His stiffness, slowness, pain and aches
His confusion, forgetfulness, his muddled-up talk
His powerless legs that refuse to walk
His unstoppable twisting and restless legs
His impossible to sit up and get out of bed
Curling toes, failing sight, these things will be put right

Not today nor this year I'm feeling,
But they'll find him, kill him and send him reeling…
So until then PD people stay strong and survive

Be ready for his downfall, stay alive
For there's hope on the horizon, we've promises galore
And we just want our lives back… nothing more

I Fell Today...

I fell today, the shocked muscles and bones now oozing pain with every stiffened movement. I am running out of limbs that are functioning only my index and middle finger are, at this time, in use. It was a knee-crunching, finger-grazing, slap-bang-on-the-ground fall, stunning my body for sure but even more so my pride. As a 57-year-old woman attempting to pull herself into an upright position opposite a supermarket I knew without looking around that I would be the focus of attention. Fleetingly, I thought to myself "This is it, how long can I continue". The constant tripping is now turning into full-blown falls. I neglect to notice the blood trickling from my finger but instantly feel the unseen graze on my knee.

As I gingerly stand upright I turn my head and glimpse a sea of faces on the opposite side of the road. One group asks "Are you okay?" I shout back "Yes I'm fine thank you". However, for one fleeting uncomfortable moment I sense a feeling I've never encountered before, silently conveying itself to me from a different group who continued their stare or was it more like a glare? Perhaps I was still in sensitive mode but I felt something akin to abhorrence wafting its way across the road. Were they, by any chance, thinking I may have partaken of a drop of intoxicating liquor while loading my groceries into the car, which in turn caused me to stumble? I felt tears begin to well in my eyes, a sudden and depressive feeling creeping through me. How wrong they would be! I wanted to shout from across the road about my illness, but I didn't.

Then, as I picked up my bags, a man got out of his parked car and shouted "Are you okay?" I replied "I'm okay thank you" and proceeded to continue on my mission, to which much later, and despite my now-discovered bleeding and bruised fingers, I managed to giggle as reality dawned that the task at hand was to a bottle bank… Oh dear, guilty by assumption. So as I continue to write this, I have one finger remaining, the other limbs shutting down through pain, stiffness and my ever-twisting Parki leg. What will greet me come morning is anyone's guess but for now, I'll say goodnight….

Constipation…on the Move or Not

Oh Movicol, Movicol, wherefore art thou Movicol
I'm drinking you down each night
One litre, eight sachets, every six hours
Yet not a motion in sight
I hear you deep down in my bowels
Gurgling a host of sounds
But alas no result to show
Yet it's there, in my colon, I know

Is it the way I rip open your packet
Living with you so long
Should I be gentler when pouring
Speak to me, tell me what's wrong
Can we not work any longer together
Have our worlds grown so far apart
Oh, something's missing because something's not giving
Perhaps we weren't meant from the start

But I was told I had to have you
They said you were the one for me
And I've been faithful, except for Senokot
Because the doc says you work better with three….
Yes, Movicol and me are divorcing
His pace of life is much too slow
I've decided to look for a plunger
Who'll make me ready, steady, go

Yellow Seats Amidst Covid Shortages

Does your toilet seat turn yellow overnight?
Do you think it's not a pretty sight?
They say "Take Stalevo, and you'll soon be alright"
But your toilet will turn yellow overnight

Does your toilet seat turn yellow overnight
Do you spend all day bleaching 'till it's white
No matter what you do the yellow just comes through
Oh will we ever get this PD working right

Does your toilet seat turn yellow overnight?
Jim's bleaching ours, but it's putting up a fight
There's no toilet seats to be had
Like the toilet rolls how sad
Perchance the Wexford branch can put it right
ha! ha!

Reflection 3

I am losing my way, and I can feel the weight of a pending dark cloud hovering, waiting for that vulnerable window so it can seep through my once harsher exterior. Through all my battles, knocks and trials, I have persevered and kept afloat, yet this illness is winning, and I long for quietude. My will, that powerful strength that puts you back up on your feet is leaving me. Like the dopamine, it has been depleted and worn down by circumstance. Enthusiasm, that golden gift that keeps you alive, that feeds your brain, involves you with life, has left me and so I retreat back into my own comfort.

All about me are words that I have changed I am not the same. Are they seeking the person I was and judging that who is no more. I have tried for too long to remain true, to be upbeat, to involve, to explain, to educate while battling this indescribable wasting, constantly pushing as hard as I can. Not wishing to put upon, begrudge, or moan in case I belittle those who go before me with more horrible afflictions, sufferings even death. I am lost in the struggle of having to force my mind to move my body, to break out of that brain fog and face the day, to struggle each morning with my vision, to finish a task without moving onto another, to try and stay awake during the day yet sleep when night falls, to cease stopping mid-sentence losing the conversation, to be unable to stand for long yet walk at full speed, to be able to control a vehicle yet at times be unable to put one foot in front of another.

These are the conflicting mysteries of PD, mysteries that to the human eye remain unseen or unfathomable. Do not hinder me then, with confrontation, worry or anxiety. Do not chain me down with visons of who I was... rather, let me fly free. For this is me a carrier and survivor of PD. I am bound by the rules of an illness, encased within its borders.

It will decide my fate, gradually moulding me to someone you will not recognise. Yet somewhere deep down there will be a part of me that remains, a small trace, a link to the past. Catch it if ever it surfaces and hold it tight within your grasp lest I disappear forever...

Don't ask me to punctuate

Don't ask me to punctuate
As my hands can get stiff and curled
And my arm types in rigid extension
In order for the letters to unfurl
Don't ask me to punctuate
My energy is near spent
Trying to gain comfort as I type
But every limb feels bent
Don't ask me to punctuate
As I grasp the ground with curled feet
My leg constantly tightening in spasm
Making it difficult to stay still on my seat
Don't ask me to punctuate
My spine feels it's losing direction
As it turns this way and that
I'm finding it hard to reach my intention
Don't ask me to punctuate if the
Words don't appear too right
It's because I'm losing power
Not because I'm not that bright
But sometimes things have to be cut short
And for me it's the only way
Don't ask me to punctuate
As I'm afraid I won't reach the end
It's hard holding myself rigid each time
So try to understand what I send
Don't ask me to punctuate
While my movements are so slow
I just need to get down the words
Only then can I relax and let go....

The Victims of PD ...

I'm writing for the silenced voices
Of the victims of PD
Describing a condition that others may not see
So many of its faces hidden from view
Too many to list a virtual queue
It starts like a lot of illnesses
From deep inside
Eating away over many years
Until he has nowhere to hide
Making his presence known in ways
At first not noticed
But they gradually appear
One by one and stick like a poultice

From the tiniest twitch in one finger
To your face taking on a stare
To being unable to write your name
Unbelievable but I've been there
To an infusion of nerves and limbs
Going against the grain
Causing havoc to your body
Driving you insane
For sixteen years I've conquered each hurdle
The best way I could
My body accepting so readily
What my mind never would
I may not make it to the finish line
I may trip and never alight
I am carrying PD on my back
And he's not a pretty sight

He makes my inner spine shake so much
I cannot stand straight
My legs feel so heavy
Making my distorted body ache
My words are stopping in mid-sentence
My face has started to frown
Yet you may think I look fine
If you saw me about the town
But like petrol in a car
Or batteries that have worn out
Everything has a shelf life
So I'm in no doubt
It will not get any better
No findings, no real cure
Just continuous surveys
From the scientists to endure

But there's a need to educate
How all-consuming PD can be
Affecting every nerve
Like the branches of a tree
Making them so weak
Throughout the day and night
The shivering, shaking
Deep in my spine hidden out of sight
Little sleep do I get through those hours
As he twists and turns me at will
Yet all I want is to close my eyes
And dream of being still
If perchance he grants me sleep
He lays waiting to pounce
I open my eyes and there he is
Zapping my strength ounce for ounce

Laughing at my efforts
As I painfully struggle out of bed
Laughing at the stiffness
That has me feeling like led
Sometimes he will give me
A window of space
Whereby I can function better
And another day face

Yet he's there, always lurking
Robbing me piece by piece
Knocking down my very existence
Willing me to cease
Finding things to meddle with
Distort, or turn around
Knocking down the very bricks
Of the life that I have found

I am tormented
By something that will not fade or heal
But instead takes over your body
And misery is all you feel
Nor will he give in
No matter what you throw
But everyone has to fight their leech
And mine's not the worst, heaven knows
I've had the Requip, Stalevo and Patches
The Rivotril, Madopar and all kinds of Sachets
I've dealt with hallucinations, shuffling and freezing
Cramps, stiffness, shouting out while sleeping
Leaning on worktops as I drag myself along
Bent forward from a back and legs
That are no longer strong

Living Beyond The Tremors

Barefoot helps me grasp the floor
As I shuffle across from door to door
The curled toes distorting my walking
The medicated brain confused whenever I'm talking
Every morning is the same
I am stiff and in pain
As slowly the rigid muscles
Twist and unwind again
My legs and back refuse to hold me still
And my balance fights against my will
Yet I struggle, shuffling forward
I cannot give in to his demands
But by the time I reach my destination
He has taken it out of my hands
How I hate this straitjacket
Wrapped tightly around my bones
That locks me within its grasp
And weighs me down with stones

What tomorrow brings
We can only wait and see
Just another symptom
To stop us feeling free
So gather us all together
And place us in a box
Leave us in a corner
Safe behind a lock
Place us bottom of a queue
As you know we can survive
Though our minds and bodies are separating
Medication will keep us alive
Yes, at times it feels
Like we're a forgotten illness

Kept and maintained by just a few
We're hanging on by threads
Not knowing what to do
I'm waiting for the next hurdle
That I'll try to overcome
Hoping it's not a tremor
Because then I feel he's won

And after that the final hurdle
When my mind may cease to recall
And I won't remember who you are
The cruellest fate of all
But until then I'll try laughing at him
Because he hasn't finished me yet
And to anyone coming up behind
It's important not to stress

Meet those symptoms, clear that hurdle,
Look back and give a smile
Carry on you're in the lead
if only for a short while
Don't waste that time worrying
Or thinking of PD
Spend that time living
As life intended to be

Share great moments with family and friends
Fill that bucket with a list 'till the end
Use each hour of freedom
Even when PD holds you tight
And you're trying to move forward
But he's pulling you back with all his might
Keep on pushing

Living Beyond The Tremors

Though you'll yearn to give in
You're tired of it all
But you can't let him win
One day they say there will be a breakthrough
Of that I really can't be sure
For decades they've spent time and money
Looking for a cure
Yet they can send people up into space
Even transplant a face
But as this disease continues
It feels they're leaving us behind
With ceasing bodies and confusing minds.

So, we will continue to live our lives together
PD and me
And play that tug-of-war game
That only each other can see
I'll push him back at every chance
And he'll pull me ever nearer
For he is set deep in my bones
That much has become clearer
He will not leave me now
He is too long ingrained
He's chipped away over the years
But the person in me has remained
And as long as I hold the power
I'll keep the worst at bay
Until one day, maybe,
They can chip that leech away…

Reflection 4

It's true when they say you don't know what it's like unless you walk in that person's shoes. The same goes for everyone living with a chronic illness much of each day lost waiting for that green light to say "go". So many symptoms are hidden from sight, some you won't even recognise as being connected but they will be and bravely you have to find ways to live with them as best you can. Whether it be short or long we have no choice but to carry on. Do not get bogged down therefore with information, lest you waste precious hours in your day. The reality is you may never even encounter many of the symptoms. Rather, deal with each hurdle as and when you meet them. I think I have jumped over a hundred of these obstacles, and yes, I've moaned and groaned somewhat but overall taking in the fact that I have entered my 17th year of PD, I'm pretty darned well used to co-habiting with him. Like a leech he clings to me, his constant weight weakening my spine making it vulnerable. But I deal with it, then tell him to go away and give me back some normality for a few hours.

But he can be nasty, keeping me up all night, twisting my leg tightly like an elastic band then letting go, spiralling it into super-sonic speed nearly whipping my body with it. I can neither sit, turn, nor lie down, the many pillows stacked around me my only comfort. He seems to know when I desire to go to the bathroom making it difficult for me to alight from the bed a simple, automatic task for most. As I struggle to sit up he pushes me back down like a yo-yo back and forth, leaving my spine trembling, each effort zapping what little energy I may have salvaged. Each attempt becomes more urgent in order to escape and make a shuffled beeline for the bathroom without losing a drop. Then comes the attempt to stand up straight and the ritual of trying to get my legs to move forward. Followed by the final act of freezing while my brain works out which is the best way to turn in order to manoeuvre onto the said item. After which I shuffle back entering my bed on both knees and throwing myself backwards.

The main thing is to take those wretched pills on time and if I'm lucky, I'll flow easily into the next three and a half hours of freedom. If I don't, there's nothing for it except to wait for Mr. Parki to bring me through a set of extremely uncomfortable neurological crap, which I will endure for up to two hours. "What's the good thing about having PD?" I'm asked. Firstly, I would say it makes you appreciative of the illness you've been given compared to other people's burdens. Secondly, giving people hope when they see you fully medicated and functioning gives you a good feeling and a reason for it all. Thirdly… well, there is no thirdly. Parkinson's is an awful disease and as I say, unless you experience it, explanations are lost to the wayside. For how do you describe an ever-changing, minute-by-minute, multi-faceted, multi-effective robbery of your existence…

A Poem While You Wait at The Airport

You saw me in a wheelchair today
I saw the frown upon your face
You were queuing through security
And it was moving at a slow pace
You mumbled to another person
I could barely catch the end
But it triggered down the line
And silent messages it did send

I immediately felt sad inside
I wanted to crawl away and hide
I felt embarrassed and I felt maligned
Silently accused of jumping the line
There was a time I could stand and wait
Shop 'till I drop then walk to the gate
Board the plane without hesitation
Without confusion or botheration

Until one day I learned my fate
A chronic illness that would make
My walking limited, my movement slow
My brain saying yes, yet my body saying no
An illness that medication would give
Enough strength to travel, time to live
But I'd need assistance along the way
In order to make it through the day

Alas… how do I help you see
This disease that is affecting me

Living Beyond The Tremors

Most times there is no outward sign
No badge around this neck of mine
No plaster, no crutches, no limbs held high
No arm in a sling to stop you questioning why
You probably fail to notice my body shake
When my back weakens if I'm left to wait

You probably don't notice my body shuffle or drop
When my legs won't carry me and I have to stop
But at certain times I will feel strong
And arise from the wheelchair and walk along
Those are the moments I feel free
yet these are the times you stare at me
So I would just like to say to those of you
Who grumble and mumble when I skip the queue

Who look down on me as I'm pushed along
Who then may see me walking and looking strong
There but for the grace of God go you
And I would gladly join the queue
If you'd only swap places and take my pain
And give me back my life again…
But this is my journey, and so I ask of you
To be patient and kind as they wheel me through

Show no annoyance, impatience, or rage
For one's life can be as fragile as a turn of a page…

Waiting in the Supermarket Queue

I waited in the queue today
Feeling that familiar inward shake
I had neglected to take my tablets
So my legs had taken on that ache
I chanced a quick look behind me
Where a row of people gathered
And my heart sank down below my knees
As I knew my movements would be staggered
I took the purse from my pocket
Placed the card in my hand at the ready
For that feeling in my legs implied
I wasn't going to be steady

As I lifted the blue-handled wire basket
My heart began to race
Stepping out to the point of no return
Could I manage the pace
I held my shopping bags tightly
But my worst fears were realised
As the groceries passed so quickly
I couldn't get them to go inside
Those bags were going this way and that
Why wouldn't they keep steady
If only someone would hold them
I wouldn't be long 'till ready

Again, I looked around hoping
Someone would come to my aid
But all I could see were impatient faces

What a picture I must have made
Those aches and shakes grew stronger
Yet I was only halfway through
When the machine dinged no more
I struggled to think what to do
I knew I had to make a move
Try to get the card into the slot
While everything was moving so fast
An easier task it was not

Then back to the packing and a turn of my head
Saw the queue growing longer
How I wish I had taken those tablets
They would have made me a bit stronger
Eventually I packed the last item
And moved towards the door
Acknowledging angrily to myself
I can't do this for much longer
Just another simple task that
May desert me soon forever
Gradually I'll lose more and more
Yes, that Parkinson remains clever

A silent intruder creeping unaware
Invading one's brain without a care
Devouring the dopamine leaving little behind
Just a confused body and a frustrated mind
But I am strong and determined
And I'll fight with what I've left
I have my sense of humour
I am not totally bereft
So listen when I tell you
Take heed from what I say

If Parkinson makes a home with you
Don't let him have his way

He hates the power of resistance
It dampens down his strength
So find that inner spirit
And stretch it to full length
Draw upon its resources
Live to the full each day
And if he raises his ugly head
Laugh and blow him away
For he has lived with me ten years or more
And another ten I will make
As I do not dwell in tears or fears
Or sorrow partake

I have laughed from that first moment
He came knocking at my door
It's my way of slowing him down
Stopping him from taking more
I know he will eventually win
And maybe it won't be so funny
But if I continue to laugh right in his face
Sure, it'll give him a run for his money

A Visit to The Doc

"How is your mood?"
I think and stare
Trying to find an answer
I gently slide into a glare
I know I should reply
She's looking at me, waiting
But my brain is somewhere else
Yet she's anticipating
Why can't I answer, why hesitate
Why can't I speak, is this to be my fate

"How is your movement?"
"Are you taking your meds?"
So many questions going around in my head
Trying to think of the words that say
What it's like living with PD each day
Would I be close, would I be right
Would she think I'm overstressing my plight
"What time are your meds?"
That same question again
Six, twelve, four and ten…

"And what happens then?" I try to think
A hard task when I've lost the link….
I woke this morning stiff and sore
Took a while before my toes touched the floor
I staggered a bit, creaky and bent
Shuffling my feet noisily as I went
I was able to shower, that part I'm aware

But the hands weren't in sync when I tried to wash my hair
And my skin remained damp as I tried and tried
To move that towel from side to side
I attempted to tidy up but my back soon felt weak
The ironing and cooking too much of a feat

When the meds kick in, I could strive forever
but my shoulders ache and it's not from the weather
A cramp in my foot, my hands kept locking
My leg still twisting, tightly shocking
Now the dark sets in again yet what have I done
And alas, a sleepless night has begun
So it goes on, my achievements are few
How I long to return to the life I knew
But I fear I cannot, it's here to stay
Once Parkinson makes his home
He doesn't go away

So I'll do my best to carry on
I'll keep taking those meds and remain strong
I'll laugh, I'll live and forward I'll go
Where it will take me I don't know
But a cure will come I live in hope
I'm a strong person, I can cope
But to ask me to write it down each day
I simply can't do, no how, no way

That part of me seems to have closed its door
My record-keeping skills are no more
I started, I tried, I moved just for a sec
Then suddenly I'm writing this poem... oh heck!
How do I explain to those doctors in white
Why I can't keep a diary yet a poem I can write

Living Beyond The Tremors

Maybe it's the creativity in the brain
That when all else is gone it strives to remain

Will they ever understand my struggles each day
Every part of my body going the wrong way
They see only the outside when meds set me free
And my limbs work together in harmony
But I'm not sad I don't feel blue
Just frustrated by the things I can't do
But life's full of twists we learn to adapt
Just wish I could record my symptoms exact

Maybe if I write them in a poem-like form
That to me would be more of a norm
Yes, that's what I'll try it'll be more fun
But its effects are ever-changing
And I haven't even begun
It's like pinning down a grain of sand
While the others wash away,
Then to keep a record
Of living with Parkinson's each day.

Reflection 5

I am fast approaching the end of my 19th year living with Parkinson's disease which is said to be the world's fastest-growing neurological illness after Alzheimer's. It has been a tough journey I have to admit. Yet, as I reflect on those years I have realised how easily we accept situations as painful or disturbing as they appear. Is it perhaps that we have lived through something far more painful prior to a PD diagnosis we just accept the next thing so calmly. Yet on balance, there are so many others whose fear and devastation given the same diagnosis can be soul-destroying. Amongst all the literature, we learn that PD can take many forms and that no two people will have the same experience. Difficult to understand how that could be, yet as I look around the waiting room I recognise some truth in what they say. Actually, living with Parkinson's is so difficult to describe I can only equate it to a twisting kaleidoscope whose independent shapes and colours blend and overlap, constantly moving and forming new patterns, just like a typical day with Parkinson's.

What are the worst everyday things about PD? I would say, slowly losing your independence. The feeling that everything you have achieved over the years, you are handing over to others bit by bit, and the painful awareness of having to depend on family even friends which can cause an ever-present tug of war between body and mind. Then you may ask "How do you live with it each day?" Well, firstly for me, it helps to think of Parkinson's as a solid entity a real person allowing myself to fight back and make him weak or strong according to my mood. No doubt there are a few who will laugh at these eccentricities of mine but the reality is PD is no easy illness, so you have to find a way to get through it using whatever methods work. Secondly, keeping a positive mind and jumping those hurdles that he continuously throws in my path. Rest assured, they will get higher and higher but I laugh at his endeavours, which makes him seem weaker. Thirdly and most importantly, one thing that remains constant and comforting are my family and friends, sharing with them memories, happy times or even ridiculous moments which, like tumbleweed, have gathered and become entwined in our lives allowing us to still feel part of things and helping us forget what this illness brings.

They remind me of those good times when I could steadily walk, when people could understand me clearly as I talked, when I didn't have to panic to get that last seat not out of greed but because to stand would make me weak. So do not discard me because I've become slow. If my family or friends leave me where would I go? Would I crawl back from life and take to the bed allowing Parki to win? No, that I would dread. Like the wall of pillows holding me in at night, he would cling to me with all his might imprisoning me within the Parkinson's repartee denied the simplistic movements that to others are free. My thoughts cannot help but stray to a time that now seems so far away when no medications were needed, no do's and don'ts to be heeded, just a thought-free body that moved without repression. A body that needed no force or aggression that could alight from a bed in the blink of an eye. What happened to me, how, and why? What incarcerated me within this PD regime? These are the mysteries that no one can understand, so we must go forward hand in hand and rid ourselves of this unwanted constriction. So stay close if you will as we continue to struggle …. we're just waiting to break this PD bubble.

Another Year Over

Another year over and still no cure
How long these symptoms can we endure
Twisting muscles and turning limbs
Failing memory versus thoughts of what might have been
Shaking, shivering, curling toes
Shuffling, stalling, anything goes
Vacated nerve endings without a goal
Toasted neurons taking their toll
Each day different, each hour new
Impossible to document, too hard to do
Just take the pills until you're again in motion
Digesting the regime of plasters and potions

Until that time, we see the doc
Six months, one year, maybe not
Cancelled again, out of their hand
So we wait but how can they understand
How much our illness has progressed
There is no measure, there is no proper test
Just questions that quiz our mind
As we shuffle forward while they watch from behind
Until an hour after the magic potion
We can climb Everest like a picture in motion
We can laugh, sing, do all kinds of things
But then the fuel runs out and you want to shout
But your body's weak from the rampage retreat
And you can't move because your brain is in defeat
Your body limp from head to feet
So, you wait and wait until you refuel that brain
An hour later, you're off again

Like a baby's first step taken too quick
The initial attempt takes a while to click
And like a bumping car, it staggers and stops
Then all of a sudden…. off you pop
You may have to stride, or you could go slow
As you can fall whichever way you go
But if you stand still your back will break

Those damaged interiors resonating the ache
If you didn't laugh you would surely weep
So I'll smile on this World Parkinson's Day and keep
A positive outlook for one more year
Making sure that old head of mine remains clear
I'll fit as much in as the fuel will take me
Every day, every three hours until it forsakes me
But to prevent this abandonment I surely pray
That those dedicated scientists will find a way
To give back to me what once was mine
The ability to move my body in time
To function as before, to be free of this weight

To live as normal without the fate
Of living a sentence in years ahead
Where I'll be confined totally to bed
Waiting for death to arrive at my door
While remembering all things in my life before
Those people who have crossed my way
Whose friendship I appreciate every day
For they have kept me lifted high
When Parki's side effects made me cry
So, for them I will try not to give in
I'll hold him back and not let him win
But time is of the essence and PD is growing stronger
I'm not sure I can hold on for much longer…

The Parkinson's Shuffle

(To whatever tune does it for You!)

I'll tell you a story you may not believe
It's about an illness that gives no reprieve
It came to me a long time ago
They called it PD and it makes you go slow

Well, it's really quite clever it gently moves in
Starts eating away at your dopamine
Like a car with no petrol
We slow down and stop
'Till we refuel with tablets
And then off we pop…

Chorus
But until then we'll shuffle and shake
Twist and fumble and our backs will ache
We'll have fidgety legs and not much sleep
And our executive function will be all in a heap…

Now the Neurologist asked me "How have I been?"
And I'm the best specimen he's ever seen!
As I don't have a tremor but have a good gait
Well make sure you close it, I think I can wait
Yes, there's stiffness and curling and failure to write
There are fidgety legs that have you up through the night
There's confusion and clutter and Lord knows what more
Sure, you'll have a grand time when he knocks on your door

Living Beyond The Tremors

Yes, slowly but surely I'm closing down
My face has grown a permanent frown
But I'll try to keep laughing until the end
And we'll all send that Parki around the bend!

Chorus
But until then, we'll shuffle and shake
Twist and fumble and our backs will ache
We'll have fidgety legs and not much sleep
And our executive function will be all in a heap…

So, let's come together and make a stand
Let's beat this disease sure it's got out of hand
We need a cure and we need it today
Let's kick that old Parki far away

Take our hand and join us today
Let's do what we can for Parkinson's Day
Because tomorrow may be a bit too late
And you all just might meet a similar fate
Now before I go, I have one thing to say
If every household spared a Euro today
A pound, a dollar, a Yen or a Ying
Imagine the research that money would bring!

Chorus
But until then, we'll shuffle and shake
Twist and fumble and our backs will ache
We'll have fidgety feet and not much sleep
And our executive function 'twill be all in a heap…

A Currant Bun...

Well this is my take on Parkinson's
My journey thus far in life
The cause of my anger, my angst and my pain
My rigidity, my slowness, my strife
But I'm thankful for the Parkinson I was given
Although I hate him so much
He seems to be slower than many
Yet he's not someone that I can trust

From one day to another, like a Phoenix he'll rise
Carrying yet another symptom that I will despise
And like a whimsical figure, he'll dance around the bed
Stopping me from moving as if I were dead
He drains my every minute, disconnecting my brain
So I wait for the medication to reconnect me again
In order to loosen my arms and legs
Before I attempt to get out of bed

But my back remains weak and help I must seek
To be able to stand on my own two feet
Shuffling to the bathroom with the help of an aid
I return to the bed, thankfully unscathed
Surrounded by pillows that lock me in tight
Sleeping upright to avoid that coffin feeling at night
And again in the morning the medication regime begins
But sometimes I can forget to take it and he wins

But I have moments of freedom, a few hours
Within each day that's when
I can be myself and Parkinson goes away
But he'll be back of that I'm sure when my hours are spent
If only he were a currant bun
And I could give him up for Lent…

In sharing these pages, I have captured the journey that Parkinson's and I have travelled together. It has taken much from me but it has also shown me a resilience I didn't know I had. Through pain, laughter, moments of despair and glimpses of joy, I have learned to live each day, not in the shadow of Parkinson's but beyond it. In fact wherever my future path may take me I will continue Living Beyond the Tremors ….

Printed in Great Britain
by Amazon